AZ Street Atlas of
BRACKNE[LL]

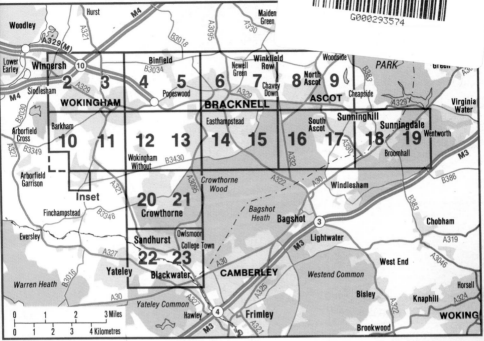

Reference

Motorway	M4	**Railway** Station, Level Crossing	**Fire Station** ■
A Road	A329	**County Boundary** + · + · + · +	**Hospital** Ⓗ
B Road	B3430	**District Boundary** — · — · —	**House Numbers** A & B Roads Only 31 22
Dual Carriageway		**Posttown Boundary** By Arrangement with the Post Office	**Information Centre** 🄸
		Postcode Boundary Within Posttown	**National Grid Reference** ↑70
One Way Street Traffic flow on A Roads is indicated by a heavy line on the drivers' left	➡	**Map Continuation** 4	**Police Station** ▲ Post Office ★
Restricted Access		**Car Park** Ⓟ	**Toilet** ▽ with disabled facilities ♿
Pedestrianized Road		**Church or Chapel** †	

Scale
1:15,840
4 inches to 1 mile

0 — ¼ — ½ — ¾ Mile
0 — 0.5 — 1 Kilometre

Geographers' A-Z Map Co. Ltd.
Head Office: Vestry Road, Sevenoaks, Kent TN14 5EP   Telephone 0732 451152
Showrooms: 44 Gray's Inn Road, Holborn, London WC1X 8LR   Telephone 071-242 9246

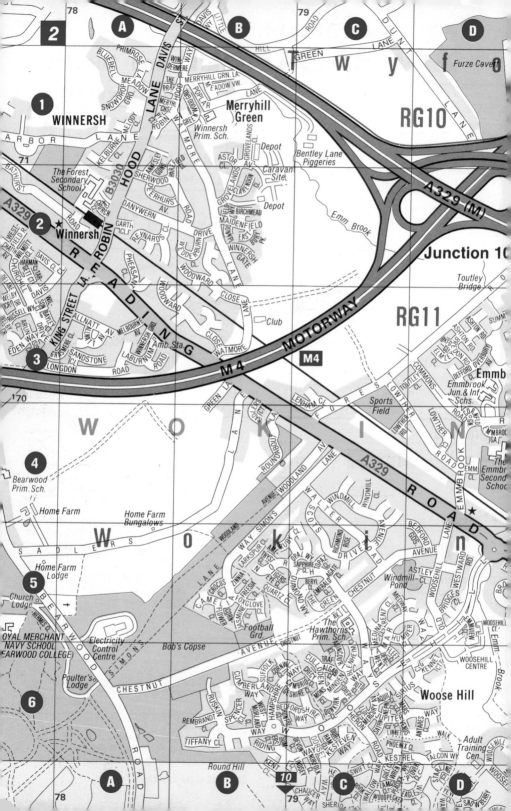

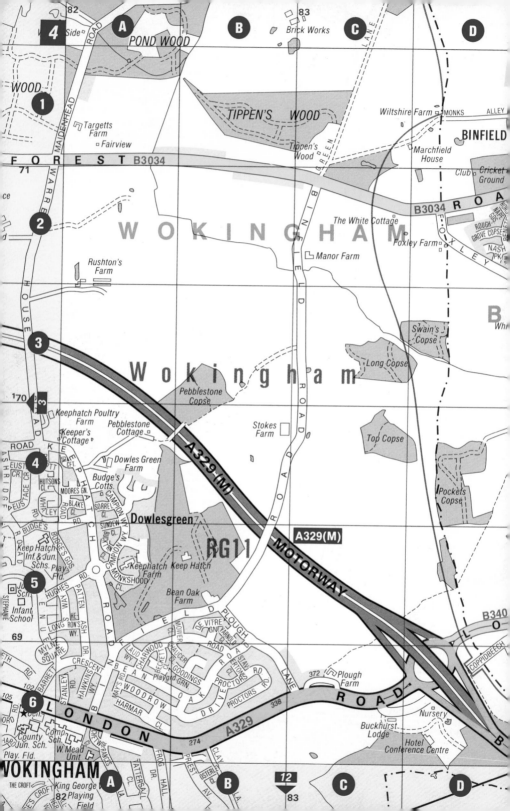

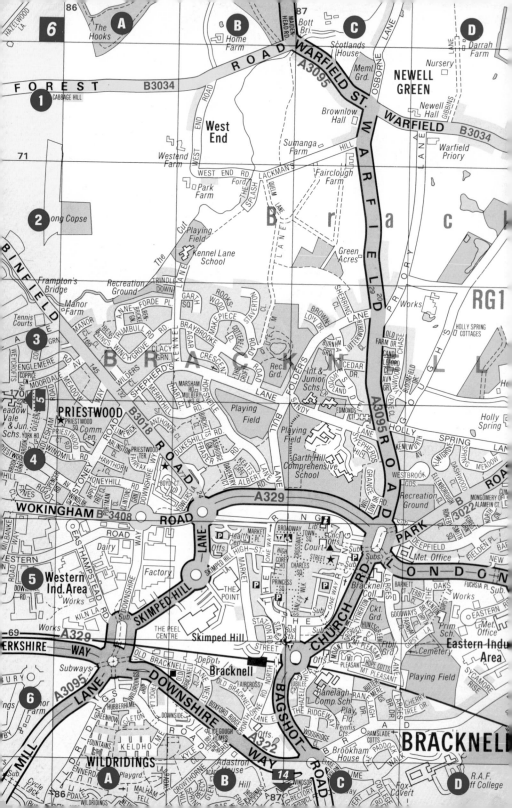

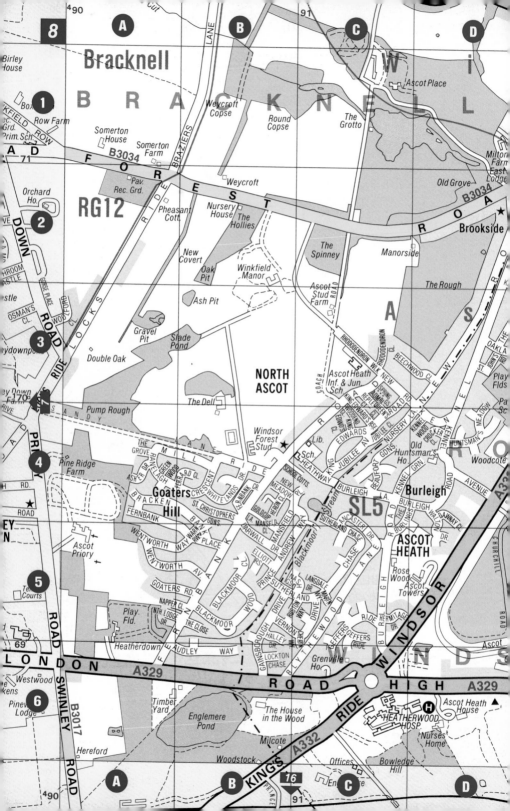

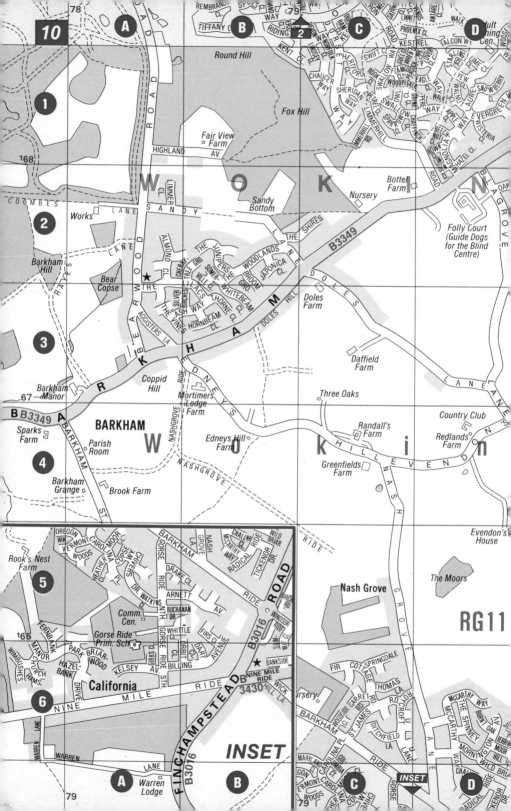

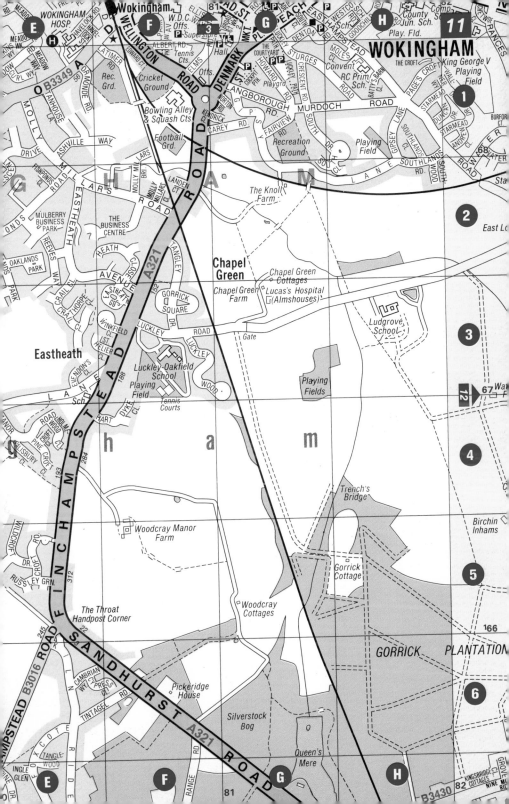

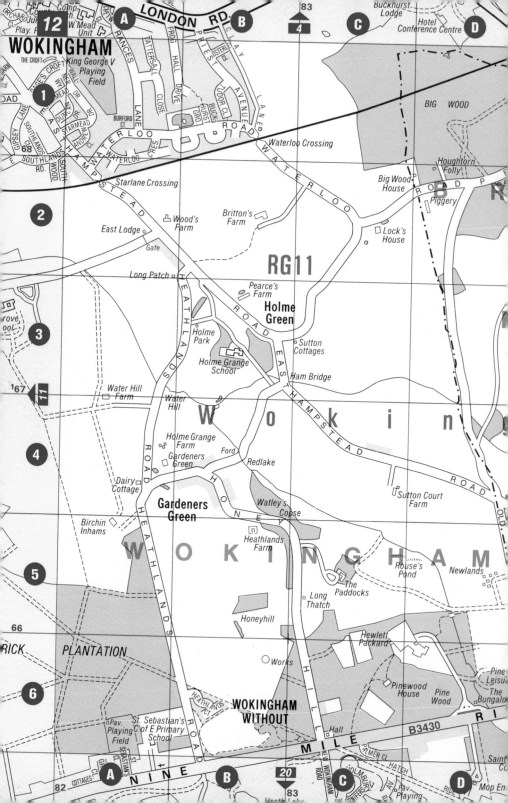

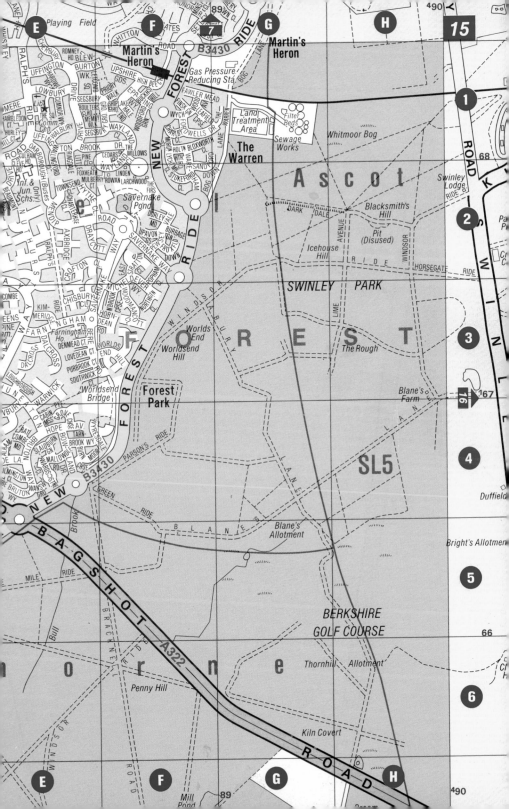

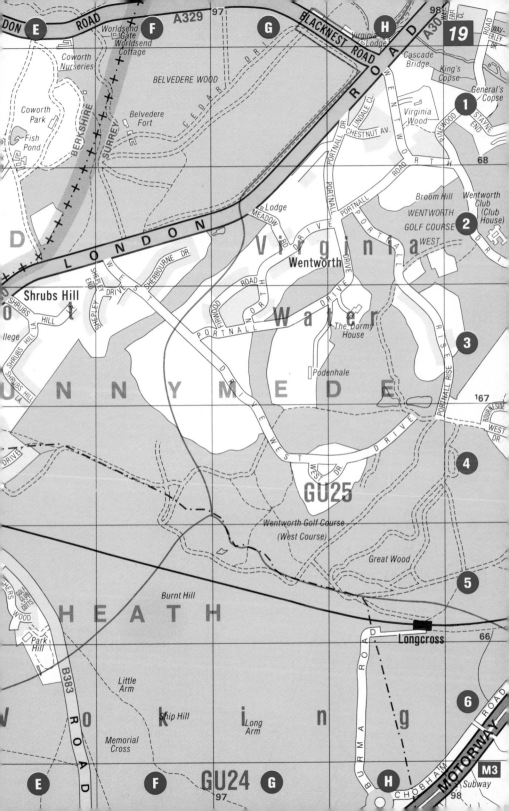

INDEX TO STREETS

HOW TO USE THIS INDEX

1. Each name is followed by its Postcode District and then by its map reference, e.g. Abbey Clo. RG11—5G 3 is in the RG11 Postcode District and appears in map square 5G on Page 3. It is not recommended that this index be used as a means of addressing mail.

2. A strict alphabetical order is followed in which Avenue, Road, Street etc., (even though abbreviated) are read as part of the name preceding them e.g. Ashdown Clo. appears after Ash Clo. but before Asher Dri.

3. Street and subsidiary names not shown on the Maps, appear in *Italics* with the thoroughfare to which it is connected shown in brackets.

GENERAL ABBREVIATIONS

All : Alley	Cotts : Cottages	Ind : Industrial	Pas : Passage
App : Approach	Ct : Court	Junct : Junction	Pl : Place
Arc : Arcade	Cres : Crescent	La : Lane	Rd : Road
Av : Avenue	Dri : Drive	Lit : Little	S : South
Bk : Back	E : East	Lwr : Lower	Sq : Square
Boulevd : Boulevard	Embkmt : Embankment	Mans : Mansions	Sta : Station
Bri : Bridge	Est : Estate	Mkt : Market	St : Street
B'way : Broadway	Gdns : Gardens	M : Mews	Ter : Terrace
Bldgs : Buildings	Ga : Gate	Mt : Mount	Up : Upper
Chyd : Churchyard	Gt : Great	N : North	Vs : Villas
Cir : Circus	Grn : Green	Pal : Palace	Wlk : Walk
Clo : Close	Gro : Grove	Pde : Parade	W : West
Comn : Common	Ho : House	Pk : Park	Yd : Yard

INDEX TO STREETS

Abbey Clo. RG11—5G 3
Abbey Rd. RG12—2D 14
Abbey Wood. SL5—4C 18
Abbotsbury. RG12—2H 13
Abingdon Clo. RG12—2E 15
Abingdon Rd. GU17—2E 23
Abury La. RG12—3G 15
Acacia Av. GU15—1F 23
Acacia Ct. RG12—1B 14
Ackrells Mead. GU17—1B 22
Acorn Dri. RG11—5G 3
Acorn Rd. GU17—5D 22
Addiscombe Rd. RG11—4E 21
Admiralty Way. GU15—6H 23
Agar Cres. RG12—3B 6
Agate Clo. RG11—5C 2
Aggisters La. RG11—3A 10
Agincourt Clo. RG11—6C 2
Alben Rd. RG12—1E 5
Albert Rd. RG11—3D 20
 (Crowthorne)
Albert Rd. RG11—1F 11
 (Wokingham)
Albert Rd. RG12—4B 6
Albion Rd. GU17—2D 22
Alcot Clo. RG11—4D 20
Aldenham Ter. RG12—3C 14
Alderbrook Clo. RG11—4A 20
Alderman Willey Clo. RG11—6F 3
Aldworth Clo. RG12—1A 14
Aldworth Gdns. RG11—3C 20
Alexander Wlk. RG12—2B 14
Alice Gough Homes. RG12—6B 6
Allenby Rd. GU15—4H 23
Allendale Clo. GU17—6C 20
Allinatt Av. RG11—3A 2
All Saints Clo. RG11—5G 3
Allsmore La. RG12—6F 7
All Soul's Rd. SL5—1E 17
Almond Clo. RG11—2A 10
Alton Ride. GU17—4E 23
Ambarrow Cres. GU17—1B 22
Ambarrow La. RG11—6A 20
Ambassador. RG12—2H 13
Amen Corner Business Pk. RG12
 —5G 5
Amethyst Clo. RG11—5B 2

Ancaster Dri. SL5—4C 8
Andover Rd. GU17—4E 23
Andrew Clo. RG11—1A 12
Angel Pl. RG12—2E 5
Anneforde Pl. RG12—3A 6
Annesley Gdns. RG11—2A 2
Antares Clo. RG11—6D 2
Apple Clo. RG11—1D 10
Appledore. RG12—3H 13
Appletree Clo. RG12—4A 6
Apple Tree Way. GU15—1F 23
Aquila Clo. RG11—6C 2
Aragon Ct. RG12—1C 14
Arbor La. RG11—1A 2
Arcade, The. RG11—6G 3
Arden Clo. RG12—5F 7
Ardingly. RG12—2A 14
Ardwell Clo. RG11—3A 20
Arenal Dri. RG11—1D 10
Arkwright Dri. RG12—5F 5
Arlington Clo. RG12—4A 6
Armitage Ct. SL5—3G 17
Arncliffe. RG12—2A 14
Arnett Av. RG11—5A 10
Arthur Rd. RG11—6E 3
Arthurstone Birches. RG12—1F 5
Arun Clo. RG11—3A 2
Ashbourne. RG12—3H 13
Ash Clo. GU17—5E 23
Ashdown Clo. RG12—5G 7
Asher Dri. SL5—4A 8
Ashfield Grn. GU17—5B 22
Ashley Dri. GU17—6E 23
Ashridge Grn. RG12—4B 6
Ashridge Rd. RG11—4H 3
Ashton Rd. RG11—3D 2
Ashville Way. RG11—1E 11
Ash Way. RG11—3B 20
Aspin Way. GU17—5D 22
Astley Clo. RG11—5D 2
Astor Clo. RG11—1B 2
Astra Mead. RG12—2H 7
Atrebatti Rd. GU17—1E 23
Audley Way. SL5—6B 8
Avebury. RG12—3A 14
Avenue, The. RG11—3D 20
 (Crowthorne)

Avenue, The. RG11—5G 13
 (Wokingham)
Avenue, The. SL5—2E 9
Avocet Cres. GU15—2F 23
Avon Gro. RG12—3C 6
Axbridge. RG12—2E 15
Aysgarth. RG12—3H 13

Bacon Clo. GU15—3F 23
Badgers Sett. RG11—3B 20
Badgers Way. RG12—4F 7
Bagshot Rd. RG12, RG11 & GU19
 —6B 6
Bagshot Rd. SL5—6F 17
Baileys Clo. GU17—6E 23
Balfour Cres. RG12—2B 14
Balintore Ct. GU15—2F 23
Ballencrief Rd. SL5—4B 18
Balliol Way. GU15—1G 23
Banbury. RG12—4E 15
Bankside. RG11—6B 10
Bannister Gdns. GU17—5B 22
Barker Grn. RG12—2B 14
Barkham Ride. RG11—6C 10
Barkham Rd. RG11—3A 10
Barkham St. RG11—4A 10
Barkhart Dri. RG11—5G 3
Barkhart Gdns. RG11—5G 3
Barkis Mead. GU15—6G 21
Barn Clo. RG12—5D 6
Barnett Ct. RG12—5D 6
Barnett Grn. RG12—3B 14
Barony Ho. RG12—4G 5
Barracane Dri. RG11—3D 20
Barrett Cres. RG11—6H 3
Bartons Clo. GU17—6A 22
Barwell Clo. RG11—3B 20
Basemoors. RG12—5E 7
Batcombe Mead. RG12—4E 15
Bathurst Rd. RG11—2A 2
Batty's Barn Clo. RG11—1H 11
Bay Dri. RG12—5E 7
Bay Ho. RG12—5E 7
Bayley Ct. RG11—3A 2
Bay Rd. RG12—4E 7
Bean Oak Rd. RG11—6A 4

Bearwood Rd. RG11—3A 10
Beaufort Gdns. SL5—4C 8
Beaulieu Clo. RG12—6F 7
Beaulieu Gdns. GU17—5E 23
Beaumont Gdns. RG12—2E 15
Beaver La. GU17—5A 22
Beckett Clo. RG11—6A 4
Beckford Av. RG12—3B 14
Beckford Clo. RG11—3D 2
Bedford Gdns. RG11—5D 2
Bedfordshire Way. RG11—6B 2
Beechbrook Av. GU17—5A 22
Beechcroft Clo. SL5—1H 17
Beechcroft Ct. RG12—6B 6
Beech Dri. GU17—6F 23
Beech Glen. RG12—1B 14
Beech Hill Rd. SL5—3B 18
Beechnut Clo. RG11—1D 10
Beechnut Dri. GU17—4D 22
Beech Ride. RG12—2D 22
Beechwood Clo. SL5—3C 8
Beedon Dri. RG12—3F 13
Beehive La. RG12—5E 5
Beehive Rd. RG12—5F 5
Bell Foundry La. RG11—3F 3
Bell La. GU17—5E 23
Belmont Rd. RG11—2D 20
Benbricke Grn. RG12—3A 6
Benetfeld Rd. RG12—2D 4
Bennings Clo. RG12—3A 6
Benning Way. RG11—4G 3
Benson Rd. RG11—3B 20
Bere Rd. RG12—3E 15
Berkshire Way. RG11 & RG12—6D
Bernersh Clo. GU17—1E 23
Berrybank. GU15—4G 23
Beryl Clo. RG15—5C 2
Beswick Gdns. RG12—4F 7
Billing Av. RG11—6A 10
Binfield Rd. RG11—2C 4
Binfield Rd. RG12—2H 5
Binstead Dri. GU17—5F 23
Birch Dri. GU17—6F 23
Birches, The. GU17—5D 22
Birchetts Clo. RG12—4B 6
Birch Gro. RG12—1C 14
Birch Hill Rd. RG12—4B 14

24 Bracknell

La. SL5—4G 7
mead. RG11—2B 2
Rd. RG11—5B 10
Side. RG11—2B 20
M. RG11—6F 3
wood Rd. GU15—3H 23
peck Pl. GU15—1G 23
dale. RG12—4G 13
opdale. RG12—1A 14
op's Dri. RG15G 3
rn Clo. GU15—2F 23
kbird Clo. GU15—2F 23
kcap Pl. GU15—2G 23
kmeadows. RG12—3C 14
kmoor Clo. SL5—5B 8
kmoor Wood. SL5—5B 8
knest Rd. SL5 & GU25—1G 19
kwater Ind. Est. GU17—5G 23
kwater Valley Relief Rd. GU15
   —6H 23

rove Dri. RG11—2D 10
rove La. RG12—2D 10
rowthorne)
ke Clo. RG11—4E 21
rowthorne)
ke Clo. RG11—4A 4
Vokingham)
ne's La. RG12 & SL5—5F 15
heim Clo. RG11—6C 2
wburton Rd. RG12—1E 15
nfield Dale. RG12—5F 5
omfield Dri. RG12—3D 6
omsbury Way. GU17—6F 23
kworth Clo. RG12—1F 15
ebell Hill. RG12—4E 7
ebell Meadow. RG11—1A 2
e Coat Wlk. RG12—2D 14
ethroat Clo. GU15—2G 23
thewood La. SL5—6C 8
en's Ride. SL5—6B 16
La. RG12—2F 15
aldish Farm Rd. SL5—2D 16
lters Ho. RG11—1E 15
ndary Vs. RG12—6G 23
rneside. GU25—4H 19
vden Rd. SL5—2G 17
ver Cres. RG11—4G 3
wland Dri. RG12—4E 15
kford Ridge. RG12—6B 6
yd Ct. RG12—4A 6
ncebridge. GU15—5H 23
scken Bank. SL5—4A 8
ckens, The. RG11—1C 20
cknell Rd. RG11—5F 15
Crowthorne)
cknell Rd. RG11—3E 21
Crowthorne)
acknell Rd. RG12—1E 7
idfields. RG12—2D 14
amblegate. RG11—2C 20
ambles, The. RG11—2A 20
amley Clo. RG11—4A 20
amley Gro. RG11—3A 20
amley La. GU17—5D 22
anksome Hill Rd. GU15—3G 23
ants Bri. RG12—5E 7
aybrooke Rd. RG12—3B 6
aye Clo. GU17—1E 23
aziers La. SL5—1B 8
edon Rd. RG11—3D 2
arwood. RG11—6A 10
ckfield Cotts. RG11—5B 20
dge Rd. SL5—2H 17
dges Clo. RG11—5D 2
dge View. SL5—4D 18
imblecombe Clo. RG11—3E 3
nn's La. GU17—5E 23
ttain Ct. GU17—3E 23
oadlands Clo. RG12—4G 5
oadlands Dri. SL5—4G 17
oad La. RG12—6C 6
oadmoor Est. RG11—4F 21
oad St. RG11—6G 3
oad St. Wlk. RG11—6G 3
oadway. RG12—5B 6

Broadway, The. GU17—2D 22
Brockenhurst Rd. RG12—6F 7
Brockenhurst Rd. SL5—1E 17
Brook Clo. GU15—1G 23
Brook Clo. RG11—4E 3
Brook Dri. RG12—1E 15
Brooke Pl. RG12—1F 5
Brookers Corner. RG11—3E 21
Brookers Row. RG11—2E 21
Brook Grn. RG12—4H 5
  (in two parts)
Brooksby Clo. GU17—5D 22
Brookside. GU17—3E 23
Brookside. RG11—5D 2
Broom Acres. GU17—2D 22
Broomfield Clo. SL5—4D 18
Broomfield Pk. SL5—4D 18
Broom Gro. RG11—2B 10
Broomhall La. SL5—3C 18
Broom Way. GU17—6G 23
Brownlow Dri. RG12—3C 6
Brownrigg Cres. RG12—2E 7
Brunel Dri. RG11—6E 13
Brunswick. RG12—4A 14
Bruton Way. RG12—4E 15
Buchanan Dri. RG11—5A 10
Buckhurst Gro. RG11—1B 12
Buckhurst Hill. RG12—1F 15
Buckhurst Rd. SL5—1B 18
Bucklebury. RG12—4A 14
Buckthorn Clo. RG11—5A 4
Buckthorns. RG12—3G 5
Budge's Gdns. RG11—5H 3
Budge's Rd. RG11—5H 3
Bullbrook Dri. RG12—4E 7
Bullbrook Row. RG12—5E 7
Bullfinch Clo. GU15—2G 23
Bull La. RG12—2F 15
Burbage Grn. RG12—2F 15
Burford Ct. RG11—1A 12
Burghead Clo. GU15—3F 23
Burleigh La. SL5—4C 8
Burleigh Rd. SL5—5C 8
Burley Way. GU17—4E 23
Burlings, The. SL5—4C 8
Burlsdon Way. RG12—4E 7
Burma Rd. RG12—6H 19
Burne-Jones Dri. RG15—4F 23
Burnham Gro. RG12—3C 6
Burn Moor Chase. RG12—4E 15
Burnthouse Ride. RG12—1F 13
Burnt Oak. RG12—6D 10
Business Centre, The. RG11—2F 11
Butler Rd. RG11—2D 20
Buttermere Gdns. RG12—6C 6
Buttersteep Rise. SL5—5A 16
Byron Dri. RG11—5D 20
Bywood. RG12—4H 13

Cabbage Hill. RG12—1H 5
Cabbagehill La. RG12—1G 5
Cabin Moss. RG12—4E 15
Cain Rd. RG12—5F 5
Calfridus Way. RG12—6E 7
Cambrian Way. RG11—6E 11
Cambridge Rd. GU15—1G 23
Cambridge Rd. RG11—6E 13
Cambridgeshire Clo. RG11—6C 2
Camelia Way. RG11—5B 2
Campbell Clo. GU17—4B 22
Campion Ho. RG12—4G 5
Campion Way. RG11—4A 4
Candleford Clo. RG12—3C 6
Cannon Hill. RG12—3C 14
Cantley Cres. RG11—4E 3
Carbery La. SL5—6F 9
Cardinals, The. RG12—1B 14
Cardwell Cres. SL5—2G 17
Carey Rd. RG11—1G 11
Carlyle Ct. RG11—4E 21
Carnation Clo. RG12—2H 7
Carnoustie. RG12—4G 13
Carolina Pl. RG11—5A 10

Caroline Dri. RG11—5E 3
Carrick La. GU17—4A 22
Carroll Cres. SL5—2D 16
Castlecraig Ct. GU15—3F 23
Caswall Clo. RG12—2E 5
Caswall Ride. GU17—5B 22
Cavendish Meads. SL5—3H 17
Caves Farm Clo. GU17—2C 22
Cedar Av. GU17—5F 23
Cedar Clo. RG11—6G 3
Cedar Dri. RG12—3C 6
Cedar Dri. SL5—1F 19
  (off Blacknest Rd.)
Cedar Dri. SL5—4C 18
  (off Broomhall La.)
Cedars. GU17—2B 22
Cedars. RG12—1F 15
Celandine Clo. RG11—2E 21
Central Wlk. RG11—6G 3
Centurion Clo. GU15—2F 23
Chaffinch Clo. GU15—2F 23
Chaffinch Clo. RG11—1C 10
Challis Pl. RG12—5B 10
Challoner Clo. RG11—5B 10
Chanctonbury Dri. SL5—4A 18
Chandlers La. GU17—2A 22
Chapel La. RG12—3E 5
Chaplain's Hill. RG11—4F 21
Charlbury Clo. RG12—1F 15
Charles Sq. RG12—5C 6
Charlton Ct. GU15—1F 23
Charterhouse Clo. RG12—2E 15
Charters Clo. SL5—2H 17
Charters La. SL5—2H 17
Charters Rd. SL5—4H 17
Charters Way. SL5—4B 18
Charwood Rd. RG11—6A 4
Chase Gdns. RG12—1E 5
Chase, The. RG11—2C 20
Chatsworth Av. RG11—2A 2
Chaucer Clo. RG11—6B 4
Chaucer Rd. RG11—4D 20
Chaucer Way. RG11—1C 10
Chavey Down Rd. RG12—1H 7
Cheam Clo. RG12—2D 14
Cheapside Rd. SL5—6G 9
Cheeseman Clo. RG11—5H 3
Chelwood Dri. GU17—1B 22
Cheney Clo. RG12—2F 5
Cheniston Ct. SL5—4C 18
Cherbury Clo. RG11—1E 15
Cherington Way. SL5—5C 8
Cheriton Clo. RG11—1E 15
Cherry Tree Clo. GU15—1F 23
Cherry Tree Dri. RG12—6D 6
Cherrytree Gro. RG11—2A 10
Chesterblade La. RG12—4D 14
Chestnut Av. GU25—1H 19
Chestnut Av. RG11—6A 2
Chestnut Clo. GU17—6G 23
Chetwode Clo. RG11—6A 4
Cheviot Rd. GU17—6B 20
Chiltern Rd. GU17—1B 22
Chisbury Clo. RG12—3E 15
Chivers Dri. RG11—5A 10
Chobham Rd. GU24—6H 19
Chobham Rd. SL5 & GU24—4D 18
Christchurch Dri. GU17—4E 23
Church Clo. RG11—2A 2
Church Hams. RG11—6A 10
Churchill Cres. GU17—5A 22
Churchill Rd. RG11—2A 2
Churchill Rd. SL5—5D 8
Church La. RG12—1G 5
Church La. SL5—2D 18
  (Sunningdale)
Church La. SL5—1H 17
  (Sunninghill)
Church Rd. GU15—1G 23
Church Rd. GU17—1B 22
Church Rd. RG11—4D 20
Church Rd. RG12—5C 6
Church Rd. SL5—1E 17
  (Ascot)

Church Rd. SL5—4H 7
  (Chavey Down)
Church Rd. SL5—3C 18
  (Sunningdale)
Church St. RG11—3D 20
Church Ter. RG12—3E 5
Circle Hill Rd. RG11—3E 21
Clacy Grn. RG12—3A 6
Clanfield Ride. GU17—5F 23
Clare Av. RG11—5G 3
Clarefield Ct. SL5—4C 18
Clarendon Clo. RG11—2B 2
Clarendon Ct. GU17—6F 23
Clarke Cres. GU15—3G 23
Claverdon. RG12—4A 14
Clayhill Clo. RG12—6F 7
Clay La. RG11—6B 4
Clayton Gro. GU17—4E 7
Cleve Ho. RG12—1E 15
Clifton Rd. RG11—4E 3
Clintons Grn. RG12—4A 6
Clive Grn. RG12—2B 14
Close, The. GU15—2G 23
Close, The. RG12—1C 14
Close, The. SL5—5B 8
Club La. RG11—3F 21
Coach Rd. SL5—3C 8
Cobbett's La. GU17—5B 22
Cock-A-Dobby. GU17—1C 22
Cockpit Path. RG11—1G 11
Coldborough Rise. RG12—4H 5
Coleridge Av. GU17—5A 22
Coleridge Clo. RG11—4E 21
College Cres. GU15—2G 23
College Rd. GU15—3G 23
College Rd. RG12—1C 14
Columbia Ct. RG11—6C 10
Commons Rd. RG11—3D 2
Compton Clo. GU17—1E 23
Compton Rd. RG12—3G 13
Comsaye Wlk. RG12—2C 14
Conifers, The. RG11—1C 20
Coningsby. RG12—1C 14
Connaught Clo. RG11—5B 20
Constable Way. GU15—4G 23
Cookham Clo. GU17—1E 23
Cookham Rd. RG12—5G 5
Coombe La. SL5—1G 17
Coombe Pine. RG12—3D 14
Coombes La. RG11—2A 10
Copenhagen Wlk. RG11—4D 20
Copperfield Av. GU15—6G 21
Coppice Gdns. RG11—3B 20
Coppice Grn. RG12—3H 5
  (in two parts)
Coppicebeech La. RG12—6D 4
Copse Dri. RG11—5E 3
Copse Way. RG11—5A 10
Corey Ho. RG12—5B 6
Cormorant Pl. GU15—3G 23
Cornbunting Clo. GU15—3F 23
Cornfield Grn. RG11—4D 2
Cornflower Clo. RG11—5B 2
Cornwall Clo. RG11—6B 2
Coronation Rd. GU17—3A 22
Coronation Rd. SL5—4E 17
Coronation Sq. RG11—5H 3
Corsham Way. RG11—3D 20
Cotswold Rd. GU17—1B 22
Cotterell Clo. RG12—3B 6
Cottesmore. RG12—4A 14
Course Rd. SL5—6E 9
Courtyard, The. RG11—1G 11
Covert La. RG12—1C 14
Covert, The. SL5—4F 17
Coworth Rd. SL5—2C 18
Cox Grn. GU15—4F 23
Crail Clo. RG11—3E 11
Crake Pl. GU15—2F 23
Crane Ct. GU15—2F 23
Cranford Pk. Dri. GU17—4A 22
Crawley Chase. RG12—2H 7
Crecy Clo. RG11—6C 2
Crescent Rd. RG11—1G 11

Crescent, The. GU17—6F 23
Crescent, The. RG12—1C 14
Cressex Clo. RG12—2E 5
Cricketers La. RG12—1G 7
Cricket Field Gro. RG11—4F 21
Cricket Hill La. GU17—6A 22
Crocker Clo. SL5—4D 8
Crocus Clo. RG11—5B 2
Croft Clo. RG11—4E 11
Crofters Clo. GU17—2C 22
Crofton Clo. RG12—2E 15
Croft Rd. RG11—5E 11
Croft, The. GU17—3A 22
Croft, The. RG11—1H 11
Croft, The. RG12—3B 6
Cromwell Rd. SL5—1F 17
Cross Fell. RG12—1A 14
Cross Gates Clo. RG12—6F 7
Cross Rd. SL5—5B 18
Cross St. RG11—6G 3
Crossway. RG12—5C 6
Crown Pl. GU15—1G 23
Crown Row. RG12—3D 14
Crowthorne Rd. GU17—2C 22
Crowthorne Rd. RG11 & RG12
　　　　　　　　　　　　—2F 21
Crowthorne Rd. RG12—2A 14
Crowthorne Rd. N. RG12—6B 6
Cruikshank Lea. GU15—4G 23
Crutchley Rd. RG11—5H 3
Culham Ho. RG12—1E 15
Culloden Way. RG11—6C 2
Culver Rd. GU15—1F 23
Cumberland Dri. RG12—4D 6
Cumberland Way. RG11—6B 2
Cumnor Way. RG12—1E 15
Cunworth Ct. RG12—3H 13
Curl Way. RG11—1E 11
Cypress Clo. RG11—6E 11
Cypress Way. GU17—5D 22

Dalcross. RG12—3E 15
Dale Clo. SL5—2C 18
Dale Gdns. GU17—2C 22
Dale Lodge Rd. SL5—2C 18
Danway Clo. RG11—4D 8
Danywern Dri. RG11—2A 2
Darby Grn. La. GU17—5D 22
Darby Grn. Rd. GU17—5C 22
Dark Dale. RG12—2G 15
Darleydale Clo. GU15—6F 21
Dart Clo. RG11—6B 10
Dartmouth Clo. RG12—6E 7
Darwall Dri. SL5—5B 8
Dashwood Clo. RG12—4D 6
Davenport Rd. RG12—4E 7
Daventry Ct. RG12—4B 6
Davis Clo. RG11—2A 2
Davis St. RG10—1A 2
Davis Way. RG10—1B 2
Deacon Clo. RG11—4G 3
Dean Gro. RG11—5G 3
Deansgate. RG12—4B 14
Deepdale. RG12—1A 14
Deepfield Rd. RG12—5D 6
Deerhurst Av. RG11—2A 2
Deer Rock Hill. RG12—3C 14
Defford Clo. RG11—3D 2
Delane Dri. RG11—3A 2
Dene Clo. RG12—3C 6
Denham Dri. GU17—5A 22
Denham Gro. RG12—3C 14
Denmark St. RG11—1G 11
Denmead Ct. RG12—3E 15
Denton Rd. RG11—6G 3
Derwent Clo. RG11—6C 2
Devenish Clo. SL5—3H 17
Devenish La. SL5—5H 17
Devenish Rd. SL5—3G 17
Devils Highway, The. RG11—3A 20
De Vitre Grn. RG11—5B 4
Devon Clo. GU15—3F 23
Devon Clo. RG11—6C 2

Diamond Way. RG11—5C 2
Dieppe Clo. RG11—6C 2
Ditchfield La. RG11—6C 10
Ditchling. RG12—4A 14
Doles Hill. RG11—3B 10
Doles La. RG11—2C 10
Dolphin Ct. RG12—1C 14
Domen Rd. GU15—6H 23
Doncastle Rd. RG12—6G 5
Donnington Pl. RG11—2B 2
Donnybrook. RG12—4A 14
Dormer Clo. RG11—3C 20
Dorset Way. RG11—6C 2
Dovedale Clo. GU15—6F 21
Downmill Rd. RG12—5H 5
Downshire Way. RG12—5A 6
　(Priestwood)
Downshire Way. RG12—6A 6
　(Wildridings)
Downside. RG12—6B 6
Drake Clo. RG11—5A 10
Drake Clo. RG12—2B 14
Draycott. RG12—2E 15
Drayton Clo. RG12—5D 6
Droitwich Clo. RG12—6D 6
Drovers Way. RG12—6F 7
Drummond Clo. RG12—4F 7
Dry Arch Rd. SL5—3B 18
Dryden. RG12—4A 14
Dukeshill Rd. RG12—4B 6
Duke's Ride. RG11—4A 20
Dukes Wood. RG11—3D 20
　(in two parts)
Duncan Rd. RG11—1H 11
Dundas Clo. RG12—1B 14
Dunkirk Clo. RG11—6C 2
Dunt Av. RG10—1C 2
Dunt La. RG10—1C 2
Durham Clo. RG11—6C 2
Durham Rd. GU15—6G 21
Durley Mead. RG12—2F 15

Eagle Clo. RG11—1C 20
　(Crowthorne)
Eagle Clo. RG11—1D 10
　(Wokingham)
Eaglehurst Cotts. RG12—1E 5
Eagles Nest. GU17—1C 22
Earleydene. SL5—5F 17
Earlswood. RG12—4B 14
Eastbury Ct. RG12—3H 5
Eastbury Pk. RG11—2B 2
Eastern La. RG11—3G 21
Eastern Rd. RG12—5D 6
East Grn. GU17—6E 23
Easthampstead Rd. RG11—6H 3 to 4D 12
Easthampstead Rd. RG12—5A 6
Eastheath Av. RG11—2E 11
Eastheath Gdns. RG11—3F 11
E. Stratton Clo. RG12—2F 15
Eddington Rd. RG12—3G 13
Eden Way. RG11—3A 2
Edgbarrow Rise. GU17—6C 20
Edgcombe Pk. Dri. RG11—3C 20
Edgedale Clo. RG11—4D 20
Edgewood Clo. RG11—1C 20
Edmonds Ct. RG12—4C 6
Edney's Hill. RG11—3B 10
Edward Ct. RG11—1F 11
Egerton Rd. GU15—4H 23
Elgar Av. RG11—1D 20
Elizabeth Clo. RG12—1C 14
Elizabeth Gdns. SL5—2F 17
Elizabeth Rd. RG11—6H 3
Ellenborough Clo. RG12—4D 6
Ellesfield Av. RG12—1G 13
Elliott Rise. SL5—5B 8
Ellison Way. RG11—6F 3
Ellis Rd. RG11—2C 20
Elmley Clo. RG11—3D 2
Elm Pk. SL5—5A 18
Elms Rd. RG11—1F 11
Elms, The. GU17—6F 23

Emerald Clo. RG11—5C 2
Emery Down Clo. RG12—6G 7
Emmbrook Ga. RG11—4D 2
Emmbrook Rd. RG11—4D 2
Emmbrook Vale. RG11—3D 2
Emm Clo. RG11—4D 2
Emmets Nest. RG12—2E 5
Emmets Pk. RG12—2E 5
Emmview Clo. RG11—5D 2
Englemere Rd. RG12—3H 5
Ennerdale. RG12—1A 14
Epping Way. RG12—1F 15
Eustace Cres. RG11—4H 3
Evedon. RG12—4B 14
Evendon's Clo. RG11—3E 11
Evendon's La. RG11—4C 10
Evenlode Way. GU17—2E 23
Everest Rd. RG11—2D 20
Evergreen Way. RG11—1D 10
Evesham Wlk. GU15—1F 23
Exchange Rd. SL5—2G 17

Faircross. RG12—6B 6
Fairfax. RG12—4A 6
Fairmead Clo. GU15—3G 23
Fairview Rd. RG11—1G 11
Fakenham Way. GU15—1F 23
Falcon Way. RG11—6D 2
Fanes Clo. RG12—4H 5
Farccrosse Clo. GU17—2E 23
Faringdon Clo. GU17—1E 23
Faringdon Dri. RG12—2D 14
Farley Copse. RG12—4G 5
Farm Clo. RG11—1E 21
Farm Clo. RG12—4H 5
Farm Clo. SL5—2G 17
Farm Cotts. RG11—4F 3
Farnham Clo. RG12—5D 6
Farningham. RG12—3E 15
Faversham Rd. GU15—1F 23
Fawler Mead. RG12—1F 15
Fencote. RG12—3D 14
Fernbank. RG11—5A 10
Fernbank Cres. SL5—4B 8
Fernbank Pl. SL5—4A 8
Fernbank Rd. SL5—5B 8
Fern Clo. RG11—1D 20
Fernhill Clo. RG12—3H 5
Fernhill Rd. GU17—6D 22
Ferrard Clo. SL5—4B 8
Fielden Pl. RG12—5D 6
Fielding Gdns. RG11—4D 20
Fielding Rd. GU15—4G 23
Fieldway. RG11—2B 2
Fincham End Dri. RG11—4B 20
Finchampstead Rd. RG11—6B 10
Findhorn Clo. GU15—3F 23
Finmere. RG12—4C 14
Finstock Grn. RG12—1F 15
Fir Cottage Rd. RG11—6C 10
Fir Dri. GU17—6F 23
Fireball Hill. SL5—4H 17
Firglen Dri. GU17—3A 22
Firlands. RG12—2C 14
Firs Clo. RG11—5B 10
Firs, The. RG12—2F 15
Firtree Clo. GU17—1B 22
Fir Tree Clo. SL5—4E 17
Firwood Rd. RG25—3G 19
Fisher Grn. RG12—2D 4
Fishers Wood. SL5—5E 19
Fishponds Clo. RG11—2E 11
Fishponds Rd. RG11—2E 11
Flamingo Clo. RG11—1C 10
Flats, The. GU17—6D 22
Fleet Clo. RG11—6C 2
Fletcher Gdns. RG12—4F 5
Flexford Grn. RG12—3G 13
Flintgrove. RG12—4D 6
Florence Way. GU15—3F 23
Folder's La. RG12—3C 6
Forbes Chase. GU15—3F 23
Fordwells Dri. RG12—1F 15

Forest End. GU17—1B 22
Forest End Rd. GU17—1B 22
Foresters Sq. RG12—6E 7
Forest Grn. RG12—4D 6
Forest Rd. RG11—3E 21
　(Crowthorne)
Forest Rd. RG11 & RG12—4C 2
　(Wokingham)　　　　　　　　to
Forest Rd. RG12 & SL5—1E 7
Fort Narrien. GU15—4G 23
Fortrose Clo. GU15—3F 23
Fosseway. RG11—3B 20
Fountains Garth. RG12—6A 6
Fowlers La. RG12—4B 6
Fox Covert Clo. SL5—2G 17
Foxglove Clo. RG11—5B 2
Foxheath. RG12—2E 15
Foxley Clo. GU17—5E 23
Foxley La. RG12—2D 4
Fox Rd. RG12—1C 14
Francis Chichester Clo. SL5—2G 17
Fraser Mead. GU15—4G 23
Fraser Rd. RG12—4B 6
Frederick Pl. RG11—6E 3
Freeborn Way. RG12—4E 7
Freesia Clo. RG11—5B 2
French Gdns. GU17—6F 23
Frensham. RG12—3D 14
Frensham Rd. RG11—2D 20
Friars Keep. RG12—1B 14
Friary Rd. SL5—3E 17
Frobisher. RG12—4C 14
Frodsham Way. GU15—6G 21
Frog Hall Dri. RG11—6A 4
Frog La. RG12—6A 6
Frogmore Ct. GU17—6E 23
Frogmore Gro. GU17—6E 23
Frogmore Pk. Dri. GU17—6E 23
Frogmore Rd. GU17—5D 22
Froxfield Down. RG12—2F 15
Fry's La. GU17—3A 22
Fuchsia Pl. RG12—5D 6
Fulbrook Clo. RG11—3E 3
Furzebank. SL5—1H 17
Furze Hill Cres. RG11—4E 21
Furzemoors. RG12—2B 14
Fydler's Clo. SL4—2F 9
Fyfield Clo. GU17—5F 23

Gainsborough. RG12—3C 14
Gainsborough Dri. SL5—6B 8
Galton Rd. SL5—3B 18
Garret Rd. RG11—6C 10
Garswood. RG12—3D 14
Garth Clo. RG11—2A 2
Garth Sq. RG12—3B 6
Geffers Ride. SL5—5C 8
Georgeham Rd. GU15—6F 21
Gibbins La. RG12—1D 6
Gibbons Clo. GU17—2E 23
Gibbs Clo. RG11—6A 10
Gipsy La. RG11—1G 11
Gipsy La. RG12—5D 6
Girton Clo. GU15—1G 23
Glade, The. SL5—2G 17
Glebeland Rd. GU15—6H 23
Glebelands Rd. RG11—5G 3
Glebe, The. GU17—6G 23
Glebewood. RG12—2C 14
Glenfield Ho. RG12—1C 14
Glenhurst Clo. GU17—6G 23
Gleninnes. GU15—1H 23
Glenwood. RG12—1D 14
Globe Farm La. GU17—5D 22
Goaters Rd. SL5—5A 8
Goldcup La. SL5—4B 8
Golden Orb Wood. RG12—4F 5
Goldsmith Way. RG11—4D 20
Golf Club Cotts. SL5—5E 19
Goodchild Rd. RG11—6H 3
Goodings Grn. RG11—6B 4
Goodways Dri. RG12—5C 6
Goose Corner. RG12—1F 7

Lanchester Dri. RG11—1E 21
Landen Ct. RG11—2F 11
Landseer Clo. GU15—4G 23
Langborough Rd. RG11—1G 11
Langdale Dri. SL5—5C 8
Larch Av. RG11—5E 3
Larch Av. SL5—2A 18
Larch Way. GU17—5D 22
Larchwood. RG12—2F 15
Larges Bri. Dri. RG12—6C 6
Larges La. RG12—5C 6
Larkspur Clo. RG11—5B 2
Larkswood Clo. GU17—1C 22
Larkswood Dri. RG11—3D 20
Latimer. RG12—5B 14
Latimer Rd. RG11—1F 11
Laud Way. RG11—6A 4
Laundry La. GU15—5H 23
Lauradale. RG12—1A 14
Laurel Clo. RG11—1D 10
Lawford Cres. GU17—4A 22
Lawrence Clo. RG11—6H 3
Lawrence Gro. RG12—4F 5
Lawrence Way. GU15—6H 23
Lawson Way. SL5—3D 18
Lea Croft. RG11—2D 20
Leacroft. SL5—2C 18
Leafield Copse. RG12—1F 15
Leaves Grn. RG12—3D 14
Leicester. RG12—4E 15
Leith Clo. RG11—1C 20
Lemington Gro. RG12—3B 14
Leney Clo. RG11—4H 3
Lenham Clo. RG12—3C 2
Leppington. RG12—4B 14
Letcomb Sq. RG12—1E 15
Lewisham Way. GU15—1F 23
Lewis Ho. RG12—3B 14
Ley Side. RG11—3C 20
Lichfields. RG12—5E 7
Liddell Way. SL5—2D 16
Lightwood. RG12—3D 14
Lilacs, The. RG11—2B 10
Lily Hill Dri. RG12—5E 7
Lily Hill Rd. RG12—5E 7
Lime Av. SL5—3H 15
Lime Clo. RG11—1D 10
Limerick Clo. RG12—4A 6
Lime Wlk. RG12—1C 14
Limmer Clo. RG11—2A 10
Limmerhill Rd. RG11—1C 10
Lindale Clo. GU25—1H 19
Lindale Rd. GU15—6F 21
Linden. RG12—2F 15
Linden Clo. RG11—1D 10
Lindenhill Rd. RG12—4H 5
Lindsey Clo. RG11—1C 10
Lingwood. RG12—3C 14
Linkway. RG11—3B 20
Linnet Wlk. RG11—6C 2
Liscombe. RG12—4B 14
Liscombe Ho. RG12—4B 14
Littledale Clo. RG12—6E 7
Lit. Hill Rd. RG10—1B 2
Lit. Moor. GU17—1E 23
Lit. Ringdale. RG12—1E 15
Llangar Gro. RG11—3C 20
Llanvair Clo. SL5—3E 17
Llanvair Dri. SL5—3D 16
Lochinver. RG12—4B 14
Locks Ride. SL5—3H 7
Lockton Chase. SL5—6B 8
Lodge Gro. GU17—4B 22
London Rd. GU20—6G 17
London Rd. RG11 & RG12—6H 3
(Wokingham)   to 4G 5
London Rd. RG11 & SL5—5D 6
(Bracknell)   to 6C 8
Longdon Rd. RG11—3A 2
Longdown Rd. GU17—1C 22
Long Hill Rd. SL5—5G 7
Long Mickle. GU17—1C 22
Longmoors. RG12—4G 5
Longshot Ind. Est. RG12—5G 5

Longshot La. RG12—6G 5
(Southern Industrial Area)
Longshot La. RG12—5G 5
(Western Industrial Area)
Long's Way. RG11—5A 4
Longwater Rd. RG12—3C 14
Loughborough. RG12—3E 15
Lovedean Ct. RG12—3E 15
Lovelace Rd. RG12—1G 13
Lovel Rd. SL4—1E 9
Lowbury. RG12—1E 15
Lwr. Broadmoor Rd. RG11—4E 21
Lwr. Church Rd. GU17—1A 22
Lwr. Sandhurst Rd. GU17—1A 22
Lwr. Village Rd. SL5—2F 17
Lwr. Wokingham Rd. RG11—2A 20
Lowlands Rd. GU17—6E 23
Lowry Clo. GU15—4F 23
Lowther Clo. RG11—4D 2
Lowther Rd. RG11—3C 2
Luckley Path. RG11—6G 3
Luckley Rd. RG11—3F 11
Luckley Wood. RG11—3F 11
Ludlow. RG12—4B 14
Lutterworth Clo. RG12—3C 6
Lych Ga. Clo. GU17—2B 22
Lydbury. RG12—6F 7
Lydney. RG12—4B 14
Lyndhurst Av. GU17—4E 23
Lyndhurst Clo. RG12—6G 7
Lyndhurst Rd. SL5—1E 17
Lyneham Rd. RG11—3D 20
Lynwood Chase. RG12—3C 6
Lynwood Cres. SL5—3A 18
Lyon Rd. RG11—2E 21
Lytchett Minster Clo. RG12—1F 15
Lytham. RG12—3G 13
Lytham Ct. SL5—2G 17

Macadam Av. RG11—1E 21
McCarthy Way. RG11—6D 10
McKernan Ct. GU17—2B 22
Madingley. RG12—5B 14
Magdalene Rd. GU15—6H 21
Magnolia Clo. GU15—1F 23
Magnolia Way. RG11—1D 10
Maidenfield. RG11—2B 2
Maidenhead Rd. RG11—1H 3
Maidenhead Rd. RG12—1B 6
Main Dri. RG12—3F 7
Mainprize Rd. RG12—4E 7
Makepiece Rd. RG12—3B 6
Malham Fell. RG12—1A 14
Mallowdale Rd. RG12—4E 15
Malt Hill. RG12—1E 7
Manor Clo. RG12—3A 6
Manor Ho. Dri. SL5—3E 9
Manor Pk. Dri. GU17—5A 22
Manor Pk. Dri. RG11—6A 10
Manor Rd. RG11—4E 11
Mansfield Clo. SL5—4B 8
Mansfield Cres. RG12—3B 14
Mansfield Pl. SL5—5B 8
Mansfield Rd. RG11—1D 10
Manston Dri. RG12—3C 14
Maple Clo. GU17—5E 23
(Blackwater)
Maple Clo. RG11—1B 22
(Sandhurst)
Maple Dri. RG11—1E 21
Maple Gdns. GU17—5A 22
Marigold Clo. RG11—1B 20
Market Pl. RG11—6G 3
Market Pl. RG12—5B 6
Market St. RG12—5B 6
Marks Rd. RG11—4E 3
Marlborough Ct. RG11—5H 3
Mars Clo. RG11—6C 2
Marshall Rd. SL5—3F 23
Marsham Ho. RG12—3B 6
Martin Clo. GU17—6F 23
Martins Dri. RG11—4F 3
Martin's La. RG12—6E 7

Martin Way. SL5—5C 8
Maryland Clo. RG11—6C 10
Mason Clo. GU17—5A 22
Mason Pl. GU17—2B 22
Matthewsgreen Rd. RG11—4E 3
Maxine Clo. GU17—1D 22
Maybrick Clo. GU17—1B 22
May Clo. GU15—2F 23
Mays Croft. RG12—1A 14
May's Rd. RG11—6A 4
Meachen Ct. RG11—6G 3
Meadow Clo. GU17—6F 23
Meadow Rd. GU25—2G 19
Meadow Rd. RG11—6E 3
Meadow View. RG11—1B 2
Meadow Way. GU17—5E 23
Meadow Way. RG11—1E 11
Meadow Way. RG12—3A 6
Medina Clo. RG11—5C 2
Medway Clo. RG11—5C 2
Melbourne Av. RG11—3A 2
Melksham Clo. GU15—1F 23
Melody Clo. RG11—1A 2
Melrose. RG12—5B 14
Membury Wlk. RG12—1E 15
Mendip Rd. RG12—2E 15
Mercury Av. RG11—6C 2
Meridian Ct. SL5—5F 17
Merlewood. RG12—2D 14
Merlin Clove. RG12—2H 7
Merryhill Chase. RG11—1A 2
Merryhill Grn. La. RG11—1B 2
Merryhill Rd. RG12—3A 6
Merryman Dri. RG11—2B 20
Merton Clo. GU15—6H 21
Metro Centre, The. RG11—2E 3
Michaelmas Clo. GU17—6A 22
Micheldever Way. RG12—3F 15
Mickle Hill. GU17—1C 22
Milbanke Way. RG12—5H 5
Millins Clo. GU15—1G 23
Mill La. GU17—2A 22
Mill La. RG12—1H 13
Mill Mead. RG11—5D 2
Millmere. GU17—3A 22
Mill Ride. SL5—4B 8
Milman Clo. RG12—5G 7
Milton Clo. RG12—3B 14
Milton Ct. RG11—5F 3
Milton Dri. RG11—5F 3
Milton Gdns. RG11—6F 3
Milton Rd. RG11—4F 3
Milward Gdns. RG12—5E 5
Minchin Grn. RG12—1E 5
Minden Clo. RG11—6C 2
Minstead Clo. RG12—6F 7
Moffatts Clo. GU17—2C 22
Moles Clo. RG11—1H 11
Molly Millars Bri. RG11—2F 11
Molly Millars Clo. RG11—2F 11
Molly Millar's La. RG11—2F 11
Molly Millars Rd. RG11—1E 11
Monks All. RG12—1D 4
Monks Clo. SL5—3F 17
Monks Dri. SL5—3F 17
Monkshood Clo. RG11—5A 4
Monks Wlk. SL5—3F 17
Mons Clo. RG11—6C 2
Montgomery Clo. GU17—2D 22
Montgomery of Alamein Ct. RG12
                              —4D 6
Moor Clo. GU15—1G 23
Moor Clo. RG11—5A 10
Moordale Av. RG12—4G 5
Moores Grn. RG11—4A 4
Moor La. RG12—6E 5
Moray Av. GU15—2F 23
(in two parts)
Morden Clo. RG12—1F 15
Mornington Av. RG11—6D 10
Mostyn Rd. RG12—3B 6
(off Merryhill Rd.)
Mountbatten Rise. GU17—1B 22

Mount La. RG12—6C 6
Mt. Pleasant. GU17—1C 22
Mt. Pleasant. RG11—6E 3
Mt. Pleasant. RG12—6C 6
(in two parts)
Mower Clo. RG11—5B 4
Mulberry Business Pk. RG11
Mulberry Clo. RG11—4E 21
Mulberry Ct. RG11—6G 3
Mulberry Ct. RG12—2E 15
Mulberry Ho. RG12—3B 6
Munnings Dri. GU15—4F 23
Murdoch Rd. RG11—1G 11
Murray Ct. SL5—2G 17
Murray Rd. RG11—6E 3
Murrellhill La. RG12—3E 5
Mushroom Castle. RG12—2H 7
Mutton Hill. RG12—4E 5
Mutton Oaks. RG12—4F 5
Mylne Sq. RG11—6H 3
Myrtle Dri. GU17—5G 23

Napier Clo. RG11—3E 21
Napier Rd. RG11—4E 21
Napper Clo. SL5—5B 8
Naseby. RG12—5B 14
Nash Gdns. SL5—5C 8
Nash Gro. La. RG11—4C 10
Nashgrove Ride. RG11—4A 10
Nash Pk. RG12—2D 4
Nell Gwynne Av. SL5—1H 17
Nell Gwynne Clo. SL5—1H 17
Nelson Clo. RG12—4E 7
Nelson Way. GU15—6H 23
Neptune Clo. RG11—6C 2
Netherton. RG12—1A 14
Nettlecombe. RG12—3D 14
Nevelle Clo. RG12—4F 5
New Forest Ride. RG12—4E 15
Newhurst Gdns. RG12—1D 6
New Meadow. SL5—4B 8
New Mile Rd. SL5—5F 9
New Rd. GU17—6G 23
(Blackwater)
New Rd. GU17—2C 22
(Sandhurst)
New Rd. RG11—3E 21
New Rd. RG12—5D 6
New Rd. SL5—3C 8
Newtown Rd. GU17—2D 22
New Wokingham Rd. RG11—1C
Nightingale Cres. RG12—2C 14
Nightingale Gdns. GU17—2D 22
Nine Mile Ride. RG11—6A 10 &
                              1A 20 to 5E
Nine Mile Ride. SL5—4C 16
Niven Ct. SL5—1H 17
Norfolk Clo. RG11—6C 2
Norreys Av. RG11—6H 3
Northampton Clo. RG12—6E 7
Northbrook Copse. RG12—3F 15
Northcott. RG12—5A 14
North Dri. GU25—3G 19
N. End La. SL5—4D 18
Northern Clo. RG12—4D 6
Northington Clo. RG12—3F 15
N. Lodge Dri. SL5—5A 8
North Rd. SL5—4H 7
North View. RG12—6E 5
North Way. RG11—5B 2
Norton Clo. RG12—6E 7
Norton Rd. RG11—1G 11
Nuffield Dri. GU15—1H 23
Nugee Ct. RG11—3D 20
Nuneaton. RG12—3E 15
Nursery La. SL5—4C 8
Nuthurst. RG12—2E 15
Nutley. RG12—5A 14

Oak Av. GU15—1F 23
Oakdale. RG12—3D 14

ene. SL5—3B 18
ngates. RG12—5A 14
Farm Clo. GU17—5E 23
eld Rd. GU17—6G 23
Gro. Cres. GU15—4G 23
ands. GU17—4A 22
ands Clo. SL5—3D 8
ands. GU17—2D 10
ands Dri. RG11—2D 10
ands Dri. SL5—3D 8
ands La. RG11—1C 20
ands Pk. RG11—2E 11
nede Pl. RG12—2E 5
, The. RG12—5D 6
ree Way. GU17—1C 22
vood Rd. RG12—5E 7
orough. RG12—1E 15
via. RG12—5A 14
Bracknell Clo. RG12—6B 6
Bracknell La. E. RG12—6B 6
Bracknell La. W. RG12—6A 6
ury. RG12—6H 5
Farm Dri. GU17—4D 22
arm Dri. RG12—3C 6
Mills Pde. GU17—3C 22
Sawmill La. RG11—2E 21
ead. RG12—2D 14
Melmore. GU17—5A 22
Wokingham Rd. RG11—4D 12
Woosehill La. RG11—5D 2
nder Clo. RG11—1B 20
r Rd. SL5—1E 17
a Ct. RG11—6F 3
ton. RG12—5A 14
ow Dri. SL5—3E 9
ow Rd. SL5—4D 18
Way. RG11—5C 2
den Way. RG12—2C 14
Clo. RG11—6A 10
ard Clo. RG11—6H 3
ard Ct. RG12—5C 6
ard Ga. GU17—2D 22
ard Pl. RG11—6G 3
on Wlk. RG11—5A 10
ital Rd. SL5—1H 17
a. RG12—5A 14
onde Rd. RG11—1E 11
rne La. RG12—1C 6
rne Rd. RG11—6G 3
an's Clo. RG12—3H 7
rley Clo. RG11—1B 12
Clo. RG11—1C 20
bury Rd. RG11—3D 2
Clo. RG11—1C 10
moor Rd. GU15—2F 23
moor Rd. RG11—6G 21
hope. RG12—1A 14
rd Rd. GU15—6G 21
rd Rd. RG11—5E 3

lock, The. RG11—2C 20
ock, The. RG12—6C 6
's Croft. RG11—1H 11
e Grn. RG11—5H 3
er Clo. RG11—6C 12
er Cl. RG11—6G 3
er School Rd. RG11—6G 3
hurst Dri. RG12—2D 14
de, The. GU17—5A 22
Av. RG11—1F 11
two parts)
Cres. SL5—3B 18
Dri. SL5—3B 18
hill Clo. GU17—6F 23
hill Rd. GU17—6F 23
land Dri. RG12—4E 7
Rd. GU17—3E 23
Rd. RG11—6F 3
Rd. RG12—5D 6
side Rd. SL5—2C 18
way. RG11—3C 20
ons Field. GU17—2D 22
on's Ride. RG12—4F 15
way, The. RG12—1E 5

Patten Ash Dri. RG11—5A 4
Peach St. RG11—6G 3
Peacock Cotts. RG12—1E 13
Peacock La. RG11 & RG12—2D 12
Peacock Wlk. RG11—1C 10
Peddlars Gro. GU17—4A 22
Peel Centre, The. RG12—5A 6
Peggotty Pl. GU15—6G 21
Pembroke. RG12—4H 13
Pembroke Clo. SL5—2H 17
Pembroke Lodge. SL5—2H 17
Pembroke Pde. GU17—4A 22
Pendine Pl. RG12—2B 14
Pendlebury. RG12—4A 14
Pensford Clo. RG11—1D 20
Penwood Gdns. RG12—3F 13
Peregrine Clo. RG11—1D 10
Peregrine Dri. RG12—2B 14
Perkins Way. RG11—1E 11
Perryhill Dri. GU17—1B 22
Perry Oaks. RG12—5E 7
Perry Way. RG12—5E 7
Peterhouse Clo. GU15—6H 21
Petrel Clo. RG11—1C 10
Pewsey Vale. RG12—2F 15
Pheasant Clo. RG11—2A 2
Phoenix Clo. RG11—6C 2
Pickering. RG12—1A 14
Picket Post Clo. RG12—6F 7
Pigott Rd. RG11—4H 3
Pine Clo. RG12—3G 23
Pinecote Dri. SL5—4B 18
Pine Ct. RG12—1E 15
Pine Croft Clo. RG11—4E 11
Pine Dri. GU17—6G 23
Pine Dri. RG11—6E 11
Pinefields Clo. RG11—3D 20
Pinehill Rise. GU17—2E 23
Pinehill Rd. RG11—4D 20
Pinehurst. SL5—2H 17
Pinewood Av. RG11—2E 21
Pinewood Rd. GU25—1H 19
Pitch Pl. RG12—1F 5
Pitts Clo. RG12—2F 5
Ploughlands. RG12—4H 5
Plough La. RG11—5B 4
Plough Rd. GU17—3A 22
Plover Clo. RG11—1D 10
Pollardrow Av. RG12—4H 5
(in two parts)
Pond Croft. GU17—4A 22
Pond Moor Rd. RG12—2B 14
Popeswood Rd. RG12—3F 5
Popham Clo. RG12—2F 15
Poplar La. RG11—1B 2
Poplars, The. SL5—2E 17
Porchester. SL5—1E 17
Portman Clo. RG12—4A 6
Portnall Rise. GU25—2H 19
Portnall Rd. GU25—2H 19
Potley Hill Rd. GU17—4B 22
Prescott. RG12—4H 13
Priest Av. RG11—1B 12
Priestwood Av. RG12—4H 5
Priestwood Ct. Rd. RG12—4A 6
Priestwood Sq. RG12—4A 6
Priestwood Ter. RG12—4A 6
Primrose La. RG11—1A 2
Primrose Wlk. RG12—2C 14
Primrose Way. GU17—1D 22
Prince Albert Dri. SL5—1B 16
Prince Andrew Way. SL5—5B 8
Prince Consort Dri. SL5—1B 16
Prince Dri. GU17—1C 22
Princess Sq. RG12—5B 6
Prior's La. GU17—5C 22
Priors Wood. RG11—4A 20
Priory Clo. SL5—4C 18
Priory Ct. RG11—1A 2
Priory La. RG12—5H 13
Priory Rd. SL5—4H 7
(Chavey Down)

Priory Rd. SL5—4C 18
(Sunningdale)
Priory, The. RG11—1A 2
Priory Wlk. RG12—1F 15
Proctors Rd. RG11—6B 4
Purbrook Ct. RG12—3E 15
Purcell Rd. RG11—1D 20
Pyegrove Chase. RG12—4E 15

Quadrant Ct. RG12—6E 7
Qualitas. RG12—5H 13
Quarry La. GU17—5A 22
Quartz Clo. RG11—5B 2
Quebec Gdns. GU17—6F 23
Queen's Clo. SL5—3C 8
Queens Hill Rise. SL5—6G 9
Queens Pine. RG12—3E 15
Queens Pl. SL5—6E 9
Queen's Rd. SL5—2H 17
Queensway. RG12—4H 5
Queen Victoria's Wlk. GU15—4H 23
Quelm La. RG12—2B 6
Quince Ct. SL5—1G 17
Quintilis. RG12—5H 13
(in two parts)

Rackstraw Rd. GU15—1E 23
Radcliffe Way. RG12—4G 5
Radical Ride. RG11—5B 10
Radnor Rd. RG12—6F 7
Raeburn Way. GU15—4F 23
Ralph's Ride. RG12—6E 7
(in two parts)
Ramsbury Clo. RG12—3G 13
Ramslade Cotts. RG12—6C 6
Ramslade Rd. RG12—1D 14
Rances La. RG11—1A 12
Randall Mead. RG12—2D 4
Ranelagh Cres. SL5—4A 8
Ranelagh Dri. RG12—6C 6
Range Ride. GU15—3H 23
Range Rd. RG11—6F 11
Range View. GU15—2G 23
Rapley Grn. RG12—3C 14
Ravensdale Rd. SL5—2E 17
Ravenswood Av. RG11—3A 20
Reading Rd. RG11—2A 2
Rectory Clo. GU17—2B 22
Rectory Clo. RG11—6G 3
Rectory Clo. RG12—1C 14
Rectory La. RG12—2B 14
Rectory Rd. RG11—6G 3
Rectory Row. RG12—1B 14
Redditch. RG12—4D 14
Red Rose. RG12—1E 5
Redvers Rd. RG12—2B 14
Redwood Dri. SL5—3D 18
Reed's Hill. RG12—2B 14
Reeves Way. RG11—2E 11
Regents Pl. GU17—2E 23
Regents Wlk. SL5—4G 17
Rembrandt Clo. RG12—6B 2
Reynards Clo. RG11—2A 2
Reynolds Way. GU15—4F 23
Rhododendron Clo. SL5—3C 8
Rhododendron Wlk. SL5—3C 8
Richmond Rise. RG11—5C 2
Richmond Rd. GU15—2G 23
Richmondwood. SL5—5D 18
Rickman Clo. RG12—3C 14
Ridge Mt. Rd. SL5—5C 18
Ridgeway, The. RG12—6C 6
Riding Way. RG11—6B 2
Ringmead. RG12—2G 13
Ring, The. RG12—5C 6
Ringwood. RG12—4H 13
Ringwood Rd. GU17—4E 23
Ripplesmere. RG12—1D 14
Ripplesmere Clo. GU17—2D 22
Rise Rd. SL5—2A 18
Rise, The. RG11—3B 20
(Crowthorne)

Rise, The. RG11—5E 3
(Wokingham)
Rise, The. SL5—3A 18
Roberts Rd. GU15—4H 23
Robin Hood La. RG11—2A 2
Robin Hood Way. RG11—1A 2
Robin La. GU17—2D 22
Rockfield Way. GU15—2F 23
Roebuck Est. RG12—3E 5
Rokeby Clo. RG12—4D 6
Roman Ride. RG11—3A 20
Romney Ho. RG12—1E 15
Romsey Clo. GU17—4E 23
Rook Clo. RG11—1C 10
Rookswood. RG12—3B 6
Rookwood Av. GU15—6G 21
Rose Ct. RG11—6F 3
Rosedale. RG12—1E 5
Rosedale Gdns. RG12—2A 14
Rosedene La. GU15—4F 23
Rose Hill. RG12—1E 5
Rosemary Gdns. GU17—5E 23
Rosemary La. GU17—4E 23
Rose St. RG11—6G 3
Rossett Clo. RG12—1B 14
Rother Clo. GU17—2E 23
Rotherfield Av. RG11—5D 2
Rothwell Ho. RG11—4E 21
Roughgrove Copse. RG12—2D 4
Roundabout La. RG11—4B 2
Round Clo. GU17—5B 22
Rowan. RG12—2F 15
Rowan Clo. RG11—1D 10
Rowan Dri. RG11—1E 21
Rowley Clo. RG12—6E 7
Royal Victoria Gdns. SL5—1E 17
Roycroft La. RG11—6C 10
Ruby Clo. RG11—5B 2
Rugby Clo. GU15—1G 23
Ruskin Way. RG11—5B 2
Russell Ct. GU17—5F 23
Russell Way. RG11—3A 2
Russley Grn. RG11—5E 11
Ruston Way. SL5—5C 8
Ryan Mt. GU17—2C 22
Ryecroft Gdns. GU17—6G 23

Sadlers Ct. RG11—4B 2
Sadlers La. RG11—5A 2
Saffron Rd. RG12—1B 14
St Andrews. RG12—3G 13
St Andrew's Clo. RG11—2B 20
St Anthonys Clo. RG12—4A 6
St Christophers Gdns. SL5—4B 8
St George's La. SL5—6F 9
St Helens Cres. GU17—2D 22
St Helier Clo. RG11—3F 11
St James Rd. RG11—6C 10
St John's Rd. GU17—3D 22
St John's Rd. SL5—3D 8
St Mark's Rd. RG12—3E 5
St Mary's Clo. GU17—2E 23
St Mary's Hill. SL5—3G 17
St Mary's Rd. SL5—4F 17
St Michael's Rd. GU17—2B 22
St Paul's Ga. RG11—5E 3
St Peter's Gdns. GU17—4A 22
St Sebastian's Clo. RG11—1A 20
Salamanca. RG11—3A 20
Salisbury Clo. RG11—4E 11
Salisbury Rd. GU17—6E 23
Salwey Clo. RG12—3B 14
Sampson Pk. RG12—4F 5
Sandford Down. RG12—2F 15
Sandhurst-Crowthorne By-Pass.
    RG11 & GU15—1G 21 & 5G 23
(in two parts)
Sandhurst La. GU17—4D 22
Sandhurst Rd. GU17—3B 22
Sandhurst Rd. RG11—5D 20
(Crowthorne)
Sandhurst Rd. RG11—6E 11
(Wokingham)

Sandown Clo. GU17—5F 23
Sandstone Clo. RG11—3A 2
Sandy La. GU17—1B 22
Sandy La. RG11—2A 10
(in two parts)
Sandy La. RG12—4C 6
Sandy La. SL5—4A 8
(Burleigh)
Sandy La. SL5—2C 18
(Sunningdale)
Sapphire Clo. RG11—5C 2
Sarum. RG12—5H 13
Sarum Cres. RG11—5H 3
Saturn Clo. RG11—6C 2
Savernake Way. RG12—3E 15
Savory Wlk. RG12—2D 4
Savoy Gro. GU17—6F 23
Scania Wlk. RG12—2H 7
School Cotts. SL5—4B 8
School Hill. GU17—1C 22
School Hill. RG11—4F 21
School Rd. RG11—6H 3
School Rd. SL5—2H 17
Scotland Hill. GU17—1C 22
Scots Dri. RG11—4C 2
Scott Ter. RG12—4E 7
Seaford Rd. RG11—6H 3
Segsbury Gro. RG12—1E 15
Selborne Clo. GU17—4E 23
Setley Way. RG12—6F 7
Severn Clo. GU17—2E 23
Sewell Av. RG11—4E 3
Seymour Ct. RG11—4A 20
Shaftesbury Clo. RG12—2D 14
Shaftesbury Ct. RG11—5H 3
Shaw Pk. RG11—5D 20
Shefford Cres. RG11—4H 3
Shelley Av. RG12—5E 7
Shenstone Pk. SL5—1A 18
Shepherds Hill. RG12—4C 6
Shepherd's La. RG12—3A 6
Shepherds Way. RG11—4A 20
Shepley Dri. SL5—3E 19
Shepley End. SL5—2E 19
Sheraton Clo. GU17—6G 23
Sherbourne Dri. SL5—2F 19
Sheridan Way. RG11—1C 10
Sherring Clo. RG12—3C 6
Sherwood Clo. RG12—5G 7
Sherwood Rd. RG11—2A 2
Shiplake Ho. RG12—1F 15
Shires, The. RG11—2C 10
Shrivenham Clo. GU15—2F 23
Shrubs Hill La. SL5—3E 19
Shute End. RG11—6F 3
Sidbury Clo. SL5—2C 18
Silver Birches. RG11—3A 10
Silver Hill. GU15—2G 23
Silwood. RG12—5G 13
Silwood Clo. SL5—5H 9
Silwood Rd. SL5—1B 18
Simkin's Clo. RG12—2H 7
Simmonds Clo. RG12—4G 5
Simon's La. RG11—6A 2
(in two parts)
Sirius Clo. RG12—4E 7
Skimped Hill La. RG12—5A 6
Slaidburn Grn. RG12—4E 15
Smith Sq. SL5—5D 6
Snowberry Clo. RG11—1D 10
Snowdrop Gro. RG11—1A 2
Somerset Clo. RG11—6B 2
Somerville Clo. RG11—2B 10
Somerville Cres. GU17—4A 22
Sonninge Clo. GU15—2F 23
Sorrel Clo. RG11—4A 4
Southampton Clo. GU17—4E 23
South Clo. RG11—6G 3
(off Peach St.)
South Clo. RG11—2H 11
(off South Dri.)
South Dri. RG11—1G 11
S. Hill Rd. RG12—3A 14
Southlands Clo. RG11—1H 11

Southlands Rd. RG11—2H 11
S. Lynn Cres. RG12—2B 14
S. Meadow. RG11—5F 21
(in three parts)
South Rd. RG11—5G 21
(Crowthorne)
South Rd. RG11—4F 13
(Wokingham)
S. View. RG12—6F 5
Southwick Ct. RG12—3E 15
Southwold. RG12—5G 13
Southwood. RG11—2H 11
Sparrow Clo. RG11—1C 10
Spencer Clo. RG11—6B 2
Spencer Rd. RG12—4H 5
Spinis. RG12—5H 13
Spinner Grn. RG12—2B 14
Spinney, The. RG11—6D 10
Spinney, The. SL5—2A 18
Splash, The. RG12—2A 2
Springcross Av. GU17—6F 23
Springdale. RG11—6C 10
Springfield Rd. RG12—4E 5
Spring Gdns. SL5—1F 17
(Ascot)
Spring Gdns. SL5—3C 8
(Burleigh)
Springhill Ct. RG12—1B 14
Spring Meadow. RG12—4D 6
Spring Woods. GU17—1E 23
Square, The. RG12—1E 15
Squirrel Clo. GU17—2D 22
Squirrels Drey. RG11—3B 20
Stable View. GU17—3A 22
Staff College Rd. GU15—4H 23
Stanhope Rd. GU15—6H 23
Stanley Rd. RG11—6A 4
Stanley Wlk. RG12—5C 6
Stanmore Clo. SL5—1E 17
Staplehurst. RG12—4G 13
Starling Clo. RG11—1D 10
Starmead Dri. RG11—1H 11
Statham Ct. RG12—4G 5
Station App. GU17—6G 23
Station Hill. SL5—6E 9
Station Ind. Est. RG11—6F 3
Station Pde. SL5—4C 18
Station Rd. RG11—6F 3
Station Rd. RG12—5B 6
Station Rd. SL5—3C 18
Staverton Clo. RG11—6B 4
Staverton Clo. RG12—3A 6
Stayne End. GU25—1H 19
Steeforth Copse. GU15—6G 21
Stephanie Chase Ct. RG11—5H 3
Stevens Hill. GU17—5A 22
Stevenson Dri. RG12—1E 5
Stilwell Clo. GU17—4A 22
Stokeford Clo. RG12—2F 15
Stoney Rd. RG12—4A 6
Stratfield. RG12—5G 13
Strawberry Hill. RG12—2E 7
Strood La. SL5—2G 9
Stubbs Folly. GU15—3F 23
Sturges Rd. RG11—1G 11
Suffolk Clo. RG11—6B 2
Summerfield Clo. RG11—3D 2
Summit Clo. RG11—5B 10
Sundew Clo. RG11—4A 4
Sunning Av. SL5—4A 18
Sunninghill Clo. SL5—1H 17
Sunninghill Ct. SL5—1H 17
Sunninghill Rd. GU20—6E 17
Sunninghill Rd. SL4 & SL5—1H 9
Sunninghill Rd. SL5—2H 17
(Sunninghill)
Sun Ray Est. GU17—2C 22
Sutherland Chase. SL5—5B 8
Swaledale. RG12—2A 14
Swallow Way. RG11—1C 10
Swancote Grn. RG12—2B 14
Swan La. GU17—3D 22
Sweetbriar. RG11—1C 20
Sweetwell Rd. RG12—5G 5

Swift Clo. RG11—1C 10
Swinley Rd. SL5—6A 8 to 6A 16
Sycamore Clo. GU17—2D 22
Sycamore Rise. RG12—6D 6
Sycamores, The. GU17—5D 22
Sydney Clo. RG11—1E 21
Sylvan Ridge. GU17—1C 22
Sylvanus. RG12—4H 13
Symondsen M. RG12—1E 5

Talisman Clo. RG11—3A 20
Tamarisk Rise. RG11—5G 3
Tamar Way. RG11—6C 2
Tamworth. RG12—4D 14
Tangley Dri. RG11—2F 11
Tanhouse La. RG11—1E 11
Tank Rd. GU15—5H 23
Tarbat Clo. GU15—2F 23
Targett Ct. RG11—2A 2
Tarnbrook Way. RG12—4E 15
Tattersall Clo. RG11—1A 12
Tawfield. RG12—4G 13
Tawny Croft. GU15—2G 23
Tebbit Clo. RG12—5D 6
Telford Av. RG11—1E 21
Templar Clo. GU17—2C 22
Tenby Dri. SL5—2H 17
Terrace Rd. N. RG12—1E 5
Terrace Rd. S. RG12—2E 5
Terrace, The. RG11—3G 21
(Crowthorne)
Terrace, The. RG11—6F 3
(Wokingham)
Terrace, The. SL5—2H 17
Theale Clo. GU15—2F 23
Thibet Rd. GU17—2E 23
Thomas La. RG11—6C 10
Thornbury Clo. RG11—3D 20
Thorne Clo. RG11—1C 20
(Crowthorne)
Thorne Clo. RG11—3B 10
(Wokingham)
Thornhill. RG12—1E 15
Thorp Clo. RG12—1E 5
Thorpe Clo. RG11—3E 11
Threshfield. RG12—2A 14
Tichborne Clo. GU17—5F 23
Tickenor Dri. RG11—5B 10
Tiffany Clo. RG11—6B 2
Tigerseye Clo. RG11—5B 2
Tilehurst La. RG12—1E 5
Timline Grn. RG12—5F 7
Tinkers La. SL5—3D 18
Tintagel Rd. RG11—6E 11
Tippits Mead. RG12—4F 5
Titlarks Hill Rd. SL5—6D 18
Toad La. GU17—6G 23
Toll Gdns. RG12—6F 7
Tolpuddle Way. GU17—5B 22
Topaz Clo. RG11—5C 2
Tottenham Wlk. GU15—1F 23
Toutley Clo. RG11—3C 2
Toutley Rd. RG11—2D 2
Towers Dri. RG11—4D 20
Townsend Clo. RG12—2E 15
Town Sq. RG12—5C 6
Trafalgar Clo. RG11—6C 2
Trafalgar Way. GU15—6H 23
Travis La. GU17—3E 23
Trent Clo. RG11—5C 2
Trevelyan. RG12—4G 13
Trindledown. RG12—2A 6
Trinity. GU15—6G 21
Trinity Cres. SL5—2C 18
Troon Ct. RG12—3G 13
Troon Ct. SL5—2G 17
Trotwood Clo. GU15—6G 21
Trumbull Rd. RG12—3A 6
Truss Hill Rd. SL5—2G 17
Tudor Clo. RG11—1B 12
Tudor Dri. GU17—6A 22
Tudor Ho. RG12—2B 14
Turnberry. RG12—3G 13

Turner Pl. GU15—4F 23
Turnpike Rd. RG12—5F 5
Tuscam Way. GU15—6H 23
Twyford Rd. RG12—4F 3
Tytherton. RG12—5C 6

Uffington Dri. RG12—1E 15
Ullswater. RG12—4G 13
Underwood. RG12—3G 13
Underwood Ct. RG12—2E 5
Union Clo. GU15—6G 21
Upavon Gdns. RG12—2F 15
Uplands Clo. GU17—2D 22
Up. Broadmoor Rd. RG11—3E
Up. Nursery. SL5—2C 18
Up. Star Post Ride. RG11—6B
Up. Village Rd. SL5—2G 17
Upshire Gdns. RG12—1F 15

Valley Cres. RG11—4E 3
Vandyke. RG12—3G 13
Venus Clo. RG11—6D 2
Vermont Woods. RG11—5A 1
Vernon Dri. SL5—5B 8
Vicarage Gdns. SL5—2E 17
Vicarage Rd. GU17—6G 23
(Blackwater)
Victoria Dri. GU17—6E 23
Victoria Rd. GU15—1G 23
Victoria Rd. SL5—2E 17
Viking. RG12—2G 13
Villiers Mead. RG11—6E 3
Vincent Rise. RG12—6E 7
Vines, The. RG11—3A 10
Vulcan Clo. GU17—3C 22
Vulcan Way. GU17—3D 22

Wadham. GU15—1H 23
Wagbullock Rise. RG12—3C 1
Walbury. RG12—1E 15
Waldorf Heights. GU17—6F 2
Waldron Hill. RG12—4F 7
Wallingford Clo. RG12—1E 15
Wallner Way. RG11—1A 12
Walmer Clo. RG11—3E 21
Walnut Clo. GU17—6A 22
Walnut Clo. RG11—1D 10
Walter Rd. RG11—4C 2
Waltham Clo. GU15—1F 23
Walton Dri. SL5—4D 8
Wanstraw Gro. RG12—4E 15
Wantage Clo. RG12—4E 15
Wantage Rd. GU15—2F 23
Ward Clo. RG11—4H 3
Wards Stone Clo. RG12—4E 1
Wareham Rd. RG12—1F 15
Warfield Rd. RG12—1C 6
Warfield St. RG12—1C 6
Wargrove Dri. GU15—2F 23
Warren Clo. GU17—2C 22
Warrendown. RG12—4G 5
Warren Ho. Rd. RG11—2H 3
Warren La. RG11—6A 10
Warren Row. SL5—5B 8
Warren, The. RG12—1G 15
Warwick. RG12—3E 15
Wasdale Clo. GU15—6F 21
Waterfall Clo. GU25—1H 19
Waterham Rd. RG12—3B 14
Waterhouse Mead. GU15—3F
Waterloo Cres. RG11—1A 12
Waterloo Pl. RG11—4D 20
Waterloo Rd. RG11—4C 20
(Crowthorne)
Waterloo Rd. RG11—1A 12
(Wokingham)
Waterside Pk. Ind. Est. RG12—
Watersplash La. SL5—4H 9
Watkins Clo. RG11—5A 10
Watmore La. RG11—1B 2
(in two parts)